THE
WRITE
MOOD

OTHER BOOKS BY ILENE SEGALOVE

Unwritten Letters

List Your Self.
(with Paul Bob Velick)

List Your Creative Self
(with Paul Bob Velick)

List Your Self for Parents
(with Gareth Esersky and Paul Bob Velick)

List Your Self for Pregnancy
(with Gareth Esersky)

List Your Self for Kids
(with Charlotte Blumenfeld)

THE
WRITE
MOOD

A Journal for All Your Feelings,
Frenzies, Rants, and Celebrations

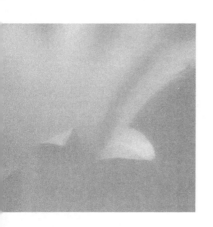

ILENE SEGALOVE

Andrews McMeel
Publishing

Kansas City

01 02 03 RDC 10 9 8 7 6 5 4

ISBN: 0-7407-0506-7

Book design by Holly Camerlinck

Rage Pages©, Blue Notes©, and Passion Sheets© used by permission from Tools With Heart, LLC, owner of the copyright.

──────Attention: Schools and Businesses──────

Andrews McMeel books are available at quantity discounts with bulk purchase for educational, business, or sales promotional use. For information, please write to: Special Sales Department, Andrews McMeel Publishing, 4520 Main Street, Kansas City, Missouri 64111.

To my dad, who was always in the mood
for any and all conversations
to illuminate, inform, or inspire,
no matter the time of day or the subject.

CONTENTS

Introduction

A dear pal calls you up and asks how you are. You launch into an exuberant "Well, I just took my car out for a long drive . . . it was beautiful . . . the sun was setting . . . I sang the whole way . . . ahhh. . . . I'm in a great mood! And how about you?" Your friend sighs, "Oh . . . it's been raining all day. . . . I've got a cold . . . and I just burned my dinner. . . . I'm in a lousy mood. I'll call you back later."

Sound familiar? Everyone has their moods. They are diverse and rich expressions of the mysterious, fickle, and captivating human condition. Moods are a mixed bag of emotion, physiology, and spirit that speaks volumes about what is going on inside each of us. They are deeply intertwined with what's on our minds and in our hearts. Since words, images, and memories enter our heads all day long, spinning and circling through the gray matter, our moods become a kind of external showcase of our ever-changing internal landscape.

We identify with our moods and often blame them for how we feel. It's as if some foreign creature takes possession of us and we find ourselves growling or grinning, depending on "its" mood. Moods can be dangerous. Saying "I'm not in the mood" too many times can lead to all kinds of arguments and even tears. "She's always so moody" sounds like a serious accusation. But moods are more than intangible entities that seem to make our days miserable or fill our hearts with warmth and hope. Moods are really reflections of who we are inside . . . parts of ourselves speaking in the form of emotions and physical sensations that if seen, cajoled, and even welcomed can enhance our lives with more meaning and more vitality.

What is it to be "in" a mood? Is it some kind of condition? Like being nearsighted, or having dandruff? Is it like being in a room with a view or stuck in some dark closet? Does it just take over? Like an internal weather system, a bossy friend, or a rash? Do we have any control over it? Should we take it seriously? And what does it tell us about ourselves?

The Write Mood puts you in the mood to embrace all of these questions. It's the right place to go to appreciate and indulge in all your many moods, and it gives you the tools and inspiration to learn more about yourself while you're at it. *The Write Mood* is a colorful journal that invites you to consider your many moods in a new light. Instead of being controlled by your many moods, you can choose to write about them instead. In doing so, you will find out what your moods are really telling you or asking of you, and then you can begin to take charge, and even change your life for the better!

The rewards of identifying a mood, writing about it, and giving it a voice are mind-boggling. You'll step outside yourself for a moment and see that you exist bigger and stronger, stripped of the limiting filter that often defines your life. The moods you don't like will not only pass more quickly, but will also give you information about what's really going on. Being blue doesn't just happen to you. When you wallow a little and immerse yourself in the blues you might be sad, whine, and wiggle, but you'll also glean an insight or two about the truth of the matter.

Writing down the hurts has a way of turning a mood around, and it can be a release. So, calm down, write, repair, and let it go. Or if you are wild with passion, celebrating a delicious success, or having a wonderful love affair, let it out on paper and make it last. When you learn to really relish your favorite moods, they'll tend to return more and more often. It's fun to think about what sends you into passion and joy or hurls you into rage or feeling blue. Imagine listing all the things that put you in a "good" mood. Here are a dozen ideas for starters:

- When the sun is shining
- Driving in my car on an empty highway singing to the radio
- Drinking coffee
- Kissing
- Listening to music
- Beauty
- Having the day to myself
- Warm apple pie
- A smile on someone's face, anyone's face
- Anything funny
- A hug from my kids
- Things going my way

It's amazing how the world seems to define how we feel. When things aren't going our way, instead of pausing for a moment and considering how we might want to respond, we often react instantly, and we fall, sometimes hard, into a spin. So many things can put us in a "bad" mood. Your list might resemble some of the following dirty dozen:

- Rain and gloomy weather
- Someone else's foul mood (moods can be contagious)
- Insomnia
- Listening to the news
- When I am careless, like losing my wallet or glasses
- When important relationships go sour for no good reason
- Being stuck in bumper-to-bumper traffic

- Lousy food at an expensive restaurant
- Paying bills, the IRS
- Not being appreciated at work
- Walking into my daughter's messy bedroom
- Not being listened to

There are probably as many moods as stars in the sky. Humans are complex beings, and daily life changes so quickly we often find our state of mind flipping back and forth from one mood to the next. Most people identify their moods as either "good" or "bad." In order to really explore what makes us tick it is useful to get slightly more descriptive. Because our lives are so up and down and in and out, the colors of our moods vary from moment to moment. *The Write Mood* reflects your ever-changing moods by giving you four different sections to write in: Rage Pages© (red), Passion Sheets© (purple), Blue Notes© (blue), and Joyous Jottings (green) cover the vast emotional spectrum that makes us human. Each section is filled with colored paper that reflects your ever-changing moods. Someone on the road might get you raging red at 9 A.M., by noon you're a passionate purple, at dusk you slip into the blues, and when midnight rolls around you suddenly find yourself joyful, vibrant green.

Say you are really angry at someone, climbing the walls with venom and fire. You can't contain yourself but you don't know what to do. Instead of lashing out on the phone to an innocent friend or driving your car way too fast, you pull out *The Write Mood* and dive into Rage Pages. Here you can unload, speak your mind, and tell it like it is. Or maybe you are just so ecstatic about something that just happened that you are quivering with delight. Then find Passion Sheets and pour out your elation.

Most people think they have little or no control over their moods.

They show up unexpectedly and leave the same way. But as you use *The Write Mood* you'll discover the benefits of paying closer attention to what's really going on. As you tune into your moods you'll see them for what they really are, a warning system of sorts. Moods tell us we need to take care of ourselves in some way. It could be a quick response to what's going on around us—perhaps our hormones are raging or we've run away too long from something that really hurts.

The Write Mood is the right place for writing about anything and everything that makes you laugh, cry, whine, scream, rant, rave, or celebrate. Moods speak a language that gives us a chance to heal ourselves. By listening and writing about what is going on inside, you'll track, illuminate, organize, and clarify who you are and who you want to be. So clean out your psychic closet and make way for the new. Since ups and downs are a normal part of life, why not ride them instead of hide them? Put it all down on paper. *The Write Mood* will help you find your way through your maze of many moods. It's an intimate road map of where you've been and where you are going.

How to Use this Book:

There are as many ways to use *The Write Mood* as there are moods in the day. It all depends on how you feel this minute. But what if you aren't exactly sure how you really feel, and maybe you just ache inside. What mood is that? You have a lot of options:

❧ Open *The Write Mood* and spend a couple of minutes gazing at the different colored pages. Let your eyes eventually settle on red, purple, blue, or green. Color is visceral; it touches your emotions in an intuitive way, and the color of a section might just invite you in. Your soul may long to be soothed by a restful blue or inspired by a vibrant green. Don't worry about what the mood is called, just begin writing on the colored paper that speaks to you.

 If you aren't sure how you feel but have the urge to just get going, turn to Passion Sheets and "List all the things you love in this world." You may start out a little slow, but after a few words you'll warm up and your list will make you feel more alive. Now if you can't find the passion, consider Rage Pages as a second potential launching pad. Scan yourself for something that irks you, some injustice or irritation you've ignored for far too long. The emotional charge from that memory is all you might need to start the wheels turning.

 If you find you long for more specific direction, or are feeling stuck, you may want to ask yourself a few simple questions:

What can't I forget about or let go of? How have I been hurt today? (Helps you identify your rage.)

What's good? What happened today that made me happy/proud/excited? (Helps you identify your passion.)

What's gnawing at me that I feel uneasy about? What am I scared about? (Helps you identify your blues.)

What feels right? Am I centered, at peace, calm? Why? (Helps you identify your joy.)

Your answers will help you identify whether you are experiencing rage, passion, the blues, or joy. As your thoughts start to percolate, turn to the appropriate mood section and begin to journal.

 You may prefer to skim through the following list of words that define an abundance of feelings. Some of the words are similar, a few show up in more than one column, but each reflects a particular nuance of temperament and disposition that is unique. Identify one that comes closest to what you're feeling at the moment. Then all you need to do is check to see which of the four moods it links up with and turn to the appropriate section. It's easy and you'll soon be on your way.

Dive into Rage Pages if you feel:

Crazed	Disgusted
Rabid	Stressed
Mean	Irritable
Grumpy	Hurt
Whiny	Fuming
Irritable	Frustrated
Enraged	Furious
Full of blame	Miserable
Out of control	Resentful
Panicked	Vindictive
Jealous	Angry
Distrustful	Agitated

Just plain out of sorts in a *loud* way

Share the sizzle with Passion Sheets if you feel:

Optimistic	Whimsical
Proud	Exuberant
Uplifted	Active bliss
Excited	Creative
Fiery	Curious
Strong	Productive
Ecstatic	Giddy
Dizzy	Lustful

Celebratory	Juicy
Radiant	Generous
Enchanted	Warm
Bright	Sensual
Playful	Kinky
Tingling	Breathless
Effusive	Courageous
Electrified	Gushy
Powerful	Loving

Just plain ecstatic in a *loud* way

Immerse yourself in Blue Notes if you feel:

Insecure	Depressed
Yearning	Confused
Hurt	Numb
Melancholy	Guilty
Wigged out	Impotent
Victimized	Suicidal
Demoralized	Ashamed
Embarrassed	Sad
Cranky	Apathetic
Anxious	Exhausted
Hopeless	Lonely
Afraid	Worried
Doubtful	Dismayed
Unappreciated	Distressed
Disappointed	At a loss
Powerless	Diminished
Withdrawn	Listless

Dull	Unworthy
Sentimental	Bottled up
Teary	Somber

Just plain out of sorts in a *quiet* way

Pour your heart out in Joyous Jottings if you feel:

Quiet bliss	Cozy
Dreamy	Loving
Glad	Rejoicing
Cheerful	Centered
Compassionate	Generous
Aware	Peaceful
Hopeful	Inspired
Enraptured	Exhaltive
Enlightened	Enchanted
Speechless	Euphoric
Wise	Satisfied
At ease	

Just plain happy in a *quiet* way

As you glance through these words, add any of your own and personalize the list with exactly what sings true for you. Then, when you need a little help, run through the list. Your own words will jump out at you and help you keep going. Remember, it's normal to feel more than one mood at a time. If you find yourself both sad and irritable you may consider writing in both Blue Notes and Rage Pages. You may also notice that as you write your mood will change. Who knows? You may begin with Blue Notes and end up in Joyous Jottings.

I'm Not in the Mood

When you aren't in the mood to write, you can be pretty sure you are hovering somewhere in the blues. That's the mood that keeps you frozen, unwilling, and unable to activate on any front. If you are sad and disconnected you'll need a little extra incentive to even find the energy to pick up a pen.

Try to give yourself permission to just go to bed, or find a little comfortable nook outside and write the following seven words in Blue Notes. "I am too sad to write today." Write this a few more times and you may find that after a little time, and a lot of compassion for yourself for feeling this way, your mood will shift ever so slightly. You might add another thought or two; that's all it really takes to break through your shell of silence and pain. You'll discover that that small amount of expression will make a little dent and allow the sun to shine through.

Some Pointers

This is not a journal of "What I did today" or a list of "Things to do." It's really a place to spill out your hopes, dreams, frustrations, and delights. You may find it useful to date your writing. After you collect a month of mood entries, you'll be able to review your feeling patterns and will begin to recognize your cycles of ups and downs. Your words will reveal a complete picture of the seasons of your life as they unfold, one day at a time.

If you are feeling blue you may want to begin your writing by reading a little of what you've already had to say in Blue Notes.

You'll remember that moods do come and go. That will help if your attitude is, "This will never end. Why bother?" Do bother. It will make all the difference.

As you write, feel free to move back and forth between moods. Feelings are not linear and they interface with one another in surprising and profound ways. There is no correct way to express yourself. Just remember, instead of trying to change your mood or hide your mood, just be your mood. It's okay to own it, wear it, write about it, and tell the truth.

The Write Mood gives you a handle on what you may have always identified as "out there," when really it's all "in here." It helps wake you up and teaches you to be more aware in your daily life. By changing your point of view you'll glean the power to explore and own yourself, all of you. So if you need to rant and rave and get it off your chest, do it! Find the red paper and rage on! Or if some fantastic fleeting feeling of sheer delight sneaks up on you, flip to the vibrant green pages and jot down the details of this unique moment of grace. Amplify your experience by making note of it. A little more joy in your life can't hurt, can it?

RAGE

PAGES

Get It Off Your Chest

Had it up to here? Been lied to? Dumped? Cut off on the free-way? Are you seething mad? If so, go for it! Rage at your boss, the IRS, your parents, and lovers past and present. Rage at anyone who's ever set you up or let you down! Rage at all of the injustices in the world and the pain and suffering that runs rampant! Follow your big red heart and rage on! You deserve to be heard!

Rage is a fiery and volatile mood, and like a force of nature, it's sometimes out of control, burning up everything and everyone in sight. Say someone just left you. No explanation. One minute he's there, the next he's gone. You are shocked, horrified, and angry. Don't waste any time. Jump into Rage Pages and make your mark. Spit it out and bare your soul. "You good-for-nothing . . . I never did trust you and now you've proven me right. How could I be so foolish? I am furious you didn't have the courage to at least . . ." Don't censor one word. Write down everything. Even if it isn't pretty.

Even though anger is uncomfortable, it is often the easiest mood to capture and write about. It almost can't wait for you to pick up your pen to start scrawling. That's because diving into Rage Pages when you're foaming at the mouth is dramatically healthy and makes a lot of sense. Somehow the wisest parts of you know that unleashing your pent-up energy lets you breathe once again. So when you are furious, frustrated, or at your wit's end, rant and rave. You'll find yourself writing big, fast, and with gusto. In no time, you'll get centered and focused enough to figure out what you need and how to take better care of yourself.

Rage Pages are red, the color of molten lava and forest fires. Let the fire of your inner fury release onto the page. Let the color red burn through the pain you feel with words that glow. You'll find working it out on paper is a very effective way to be true to yourself. You'll get to say and feel what is really important, and as a result you'll feel better, act kinder, and know a little more the next time you're lied to, dissed, or simply ignored. Life is often unfair, but that doesn't mean you have to store up your pain and accept the unacceptable. Your values deserve to be honored. So tell it like it is. Use Rage Pages as the place to scribble, scream, and speak your mind. Then step back into life and feel better for it.

To help you get started, you may want to consider these samples:

> This is driving me absolutely nuts . . .
>
> I've had it up to here with all of your . . .
>
> I'm going to finally blurt out the truth and stop
>
> > protecting you from . . .
>
> How could you lie to me, you . . .
>
> I am so furious I could just . . .

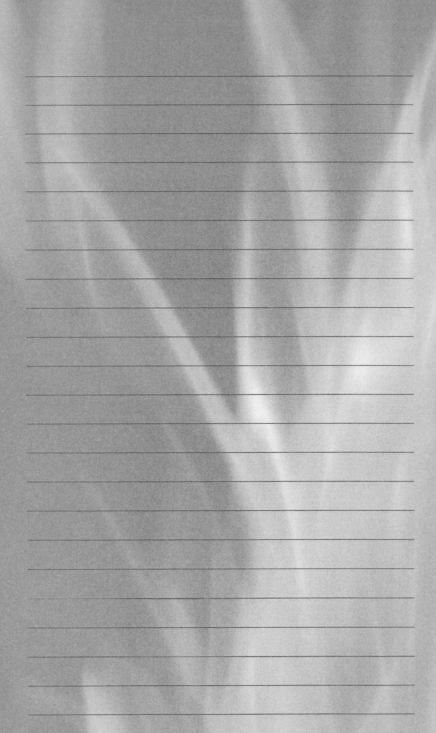

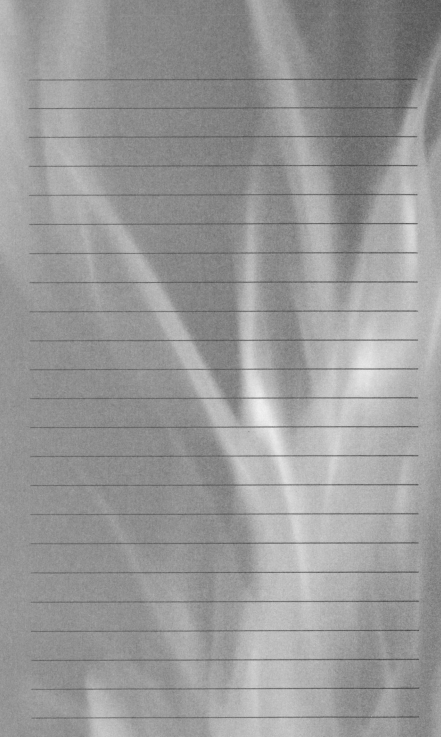

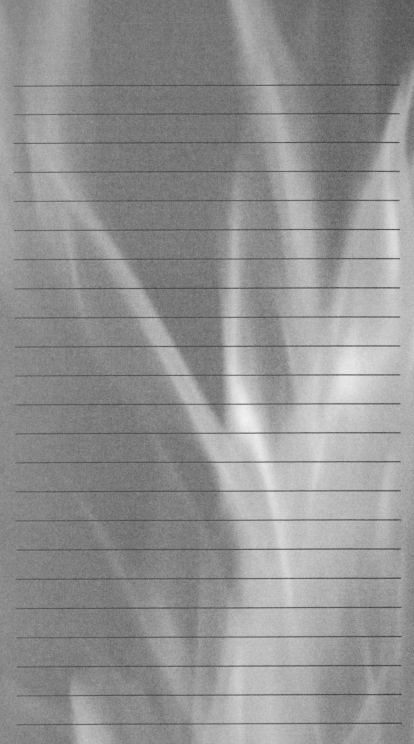

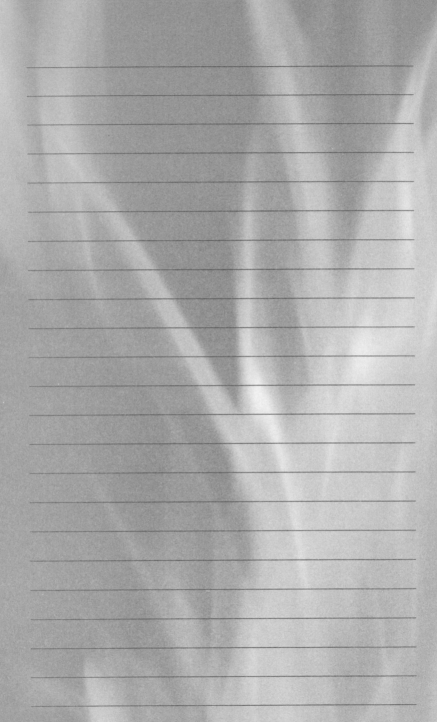

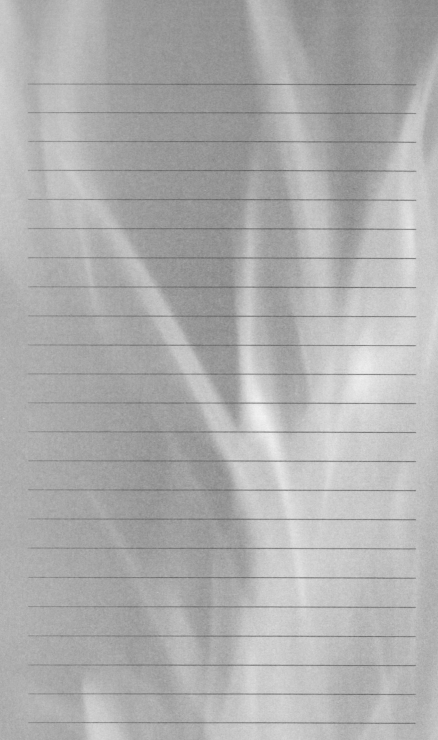

PASSION

SHEETS

Celebrate Your Best

Life is good. You've just accomplished something brilliant, made a connection that smacks of possibilities, ate the best cheesecake ever, or went on a date that made you giddy. All the glorious, euphoric moments that make life worth living spell passion. Passion feeds our very soul. It's a favorite mood, one we happily surrender to. Whether we're moved by the thrill of skiing, the beauty of nature, or the deep value of some social or political cause, everything suddenly seems to make sense, and we feel deeply intertwined with the glowing pulse of life.

Passion is usually easy to identify. It often reveals itself in our bodies. We may find ourselves breathless, our cheeks flushed, or our hearts beating furiously. Powerful as it might seem, passion often seems so fleeting. One minute we are spinning with excitement and then, all of a sudden, the fun is gone! Writing down your best is a great way to savor your passion. Just for a few moments, make a note of what happened. Get down everything you can and keep your passion alive.

Maybe you just made eye contact with an incredible stranger at a party. Somehow that one look filled you with desire. You go home, can't seem to fall asleep, and decide to unreel the story behind your quickened pulse. You write a little about walking into that crowded room and noticing that special person. As you write you settle into a deeper sense of delight, the words flow, and you connect with an enchanted part of yourself you rarely get to touch.

Reflecting on a passionate moment is great food for thought and great material for your journal. But if you aren't quite that cerebral and wonder what else to write about, make sure you give yourself permission to write about it all. Passion is a big, juicy subject. It permeates everything, including the sexy, lustful, and illicit. Let yourself go. Write about what gives you pleasure, what you love, and what you treasure. Keep track of all of your epiphanies, the unexpected and the miraculous. Make your writing a physical experience. Engage in it. Create words for feelings you've never known before. Go wild if you must. Write fast and furious or slow down and linger awhile.

Celebrate the highlights of your life and court your passion by taking pen to purple Passion Sheets. Purple is the color of royalty and enlightenment. The richness of its tone will embrace your escapades with the elegance and spirit they deserve. Collect all the dazzling people, places, and conquests that make your life particularly remarkable! This is the stuff you'll never want to forget! And be prepared for the results. You see, the more you write about passion, the more you'll have. Cultivate an active relationship with that glowing part of you that just can't wait for another bolt of insight or blast of outrageousness. Your life will be richer for it.

To help get your started you may want to reflect on these ideas:

I forgot how great it feels when I . . .

I can hardly describe the exquisite way . . .

This feeling of aliveness is something I never want to forget . . .

I can't believe what happened last night . . .

All of a sudden I was overcome with this sensation . . .

BLUE

NOTES

Soothe Your Aching Soul

Down in the dumps? Lost at sea? Lonesome or confused? You've got the blues, a state of being that's impossible to ignore. Everyone knows the blues. It shows up as a lump in your throat, tears and sighs, or just plain exhaustion. It's a mood of many nuances and degrees. It can hit us as a temporary disappointment that passes rather quickly, or can consume us with deep grief and hopelessness. Sometimes it pushes us to our limit, and we throw our hands up in the air and just want to give up. Filled with despair and frustration, we instinctively long to retreat, curl up in a corner, and pray we disappear.

As bad as it feels, being blue has an up side. It provides a buffer between us and what hurts, and gives us the time and the chance to pull ourselves together again and heal a little. But how? You might just sit in a chair awhile, breathe quietly, and wait. You can weep, wail, shake, hide, and write.

Blue Notes is the place to go when you need a safe port to drop anchor. Here you can rest, organize your thoughts, spill out your guts, and in time, find your way. Sometimes we lose faith in ourselves and others. Say you've just tried to patch up a shaky relationship. You did everything you could and still you have to admit it's going to end. You might feel like you don't have any ground to stand on. Hanging by a thin thread, your discomfort may easily turn into serious fear and loathing. But this is when the act of writing can save you. Making the move out of the darkness onto the page is a profound act of courage. It's like you're drowning, someone throws you a life vest, and suddenly your head is above water. Putting pen to paper will give you the chance to breathe again, reconnect with yourself, and feel more balance, hope, and plain relief.

So leave behind your armor and protective shell and rest for a while in the safe haven of the page. Step into Blue Notes as you might a warm bath. Immerse yourself in the soothing blue as you wash away your tears. Float a little while, pour your heart out, and watch doubt disappear. Just keep writing and you'll find yourself sorting things out, moving through confusion, and remembering that there are a lot of good reasons to get back into life.

To help you get started you might want to tap into these feelings:

I am so sad and lonely today . . .

This emptiness hurts . . .

I feel like I'll never be myself again . . .

There's no way out of this darkness . . .

I'm so afraid . . .

JOYOUS

JOTTINGS

Savor the Moments

Joy is a mysterious and wonderful mood. Sometimes it sneaks up ever so gently and we find ourselves grinning for no apparent reason. Or in the midst of watching a dazzling sunset or listening to a beautiful piece of music we're overcome by a deep sense of awe and wonder. We get goose bumps, quiver, and melt into the moment.

Joy isn't always subtle. It can hit us over the head, knock our socks off, or bring us to our knees, laughing so hard we cry. Out of thin air something shifts, and we find ourselves hovering in a glorious state of exhaltation. Some people believe joy is a divine gift, a state of grace, a closer connection with that part of ourselves more vast than our everyday identity. No matter the rhyme or reason, joy is a powerful state. Maybe joy is the ultimate mood, one that soothes and inspires, holding us, if only for a moment, in an unforgettable state of well-being.

Joy is a mood that usually employs fewer words and more feeling, so writing about it might be a little bit of a challenge. Say you've just attended the eightieth birthday party of a favorite uncle. Right when you were leaving he reminded you about a very private and meaningful moment that took place decades ago. You find yourself overcome with joy, tears fill your eyes, and you find yourself speechless. When you are angry, you are rarely at a loss for something to say. But when you are elated, or in a deep state of peace you might find yourself simply without words. So if you're lucky enough to be swept up in a joyous moment, feel your heart fill up with pleasure, make sure you enjoy, giggle, gush, and then at some point later on, explore all the marvelous sensations by filling up the page.

You'll be amazed at the results. As you write, you may discover there's more poetry than prose pouring onto the page. You see, joy infuses your mind and heart with a special feeling. The process of mindfully thinking about something that makes you joyous—be it the sound of the ocean or the taste of a great cup of coffee—will take you to a remarkable place inside yourself, a place you'll want to return to over and over again.

So don't let joy slip by. Pause, write a little, and rekindle its spirit. Fill up the glowing green pages with whatever comes to mind, be it one single word, an inkling or two, or a complete stream of consciousness. Green is the color of growth, hope, and renewal. Let the color of the pages nourish your joy and return to your writing often to remind yourself how good it feels to simply be alive.

To help you get started you may want to melt into these moments:
    This feeling of peace just welled up from inside of me and . . .
    For one moment I felt silent and wise . . .
    The joy of seeing him again was overwhelming . . .
    I opened up my heart and let in all the beauty of the
        moment . . .
    Somehow everything was perfect and I could rest again . . .